DINOSAURS™

K KAPPA Books

Visit us at www.kappapublishing.com/kappabooks

W9-CFC-332

Box-A-Dactalus

Take turns with a friend drawing a line from dot to dot. Each time an empty box is completed you receive one point. When a box has the following dinosaur you will receive the following points:

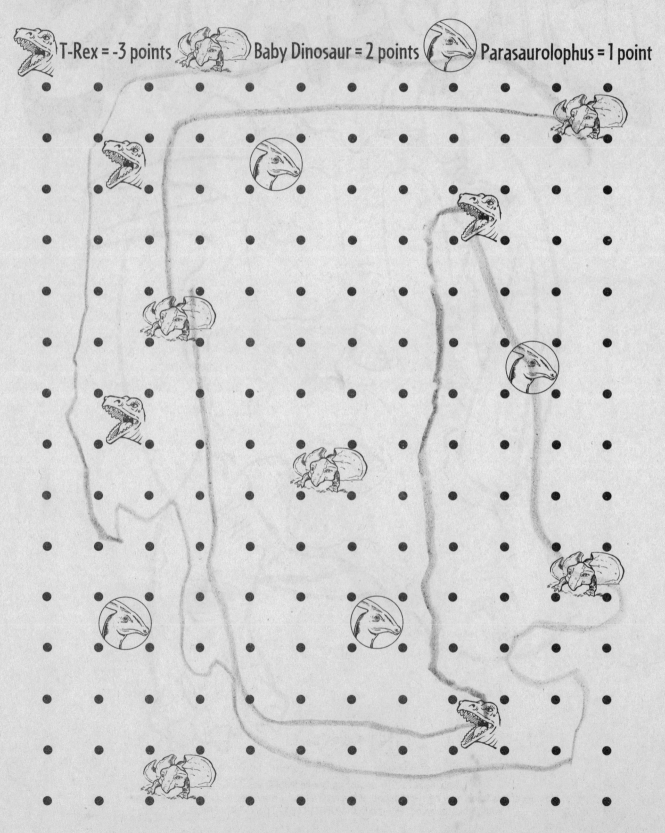

T-Rex = -3 points   Baby Dinosaur = 2 points   Parasaurolophus = 1 point

Tri-Circle-Tops

Circle the dinosaurs that are carnivores.

Crossout-Adon

Cross out the letters in the grid that appear 4 or more times. Write the remaining letters on the lines below to answer the following question:

Which dinosaur could grow to 45 feet long and 13 feet high?

T	G	M	C	H	Y	L	Z	W	P
H	R	P	L	W	Z	M	A	L	P
L	Z	H	N	G	C	N	L	H	W
H	M	O	L	S	W	H	Z	P	A
U	H	G	C	L	H	P	L	R	P
C	L	Z	U	M	S	P	H	C	Z
Z	R	M	L	H	L	G	E	P	P
L	C	H	Z	X	W	M	L	G	H

_ _ _ _ _ _ _ _ _ _ _ _ _

_ _ _

Fact-A-Dactyl

Match each dinosaur to its fact.

1. "My name means 'arm lizard'."

2. "I have a wing span of 40 feet!"

3. "I have a long neck and paddle-shaped flippers."

4. "I may be small, but I have very sharp claws!"

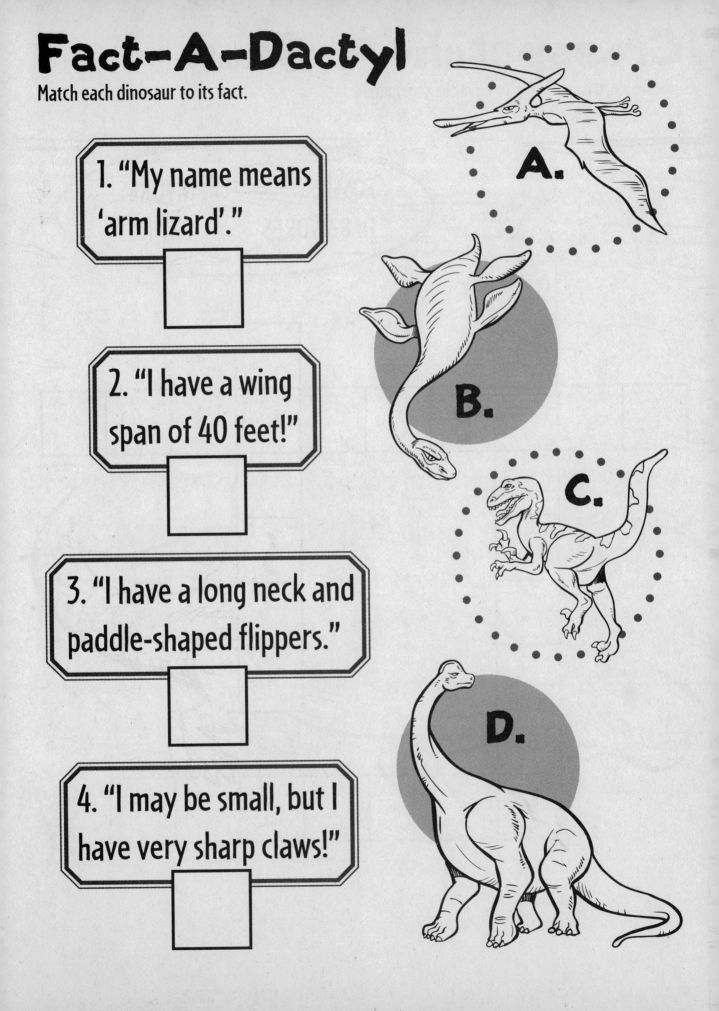

A.

B.

C.

D.

Crosspatch-A-Saur

Use the word bank below to fill in the crosspatch.

FOSSIL   CARNIVORES

HERBIVORES   EXTINCT

Which-A-Saurus

Which dinosaur does not match the rest?

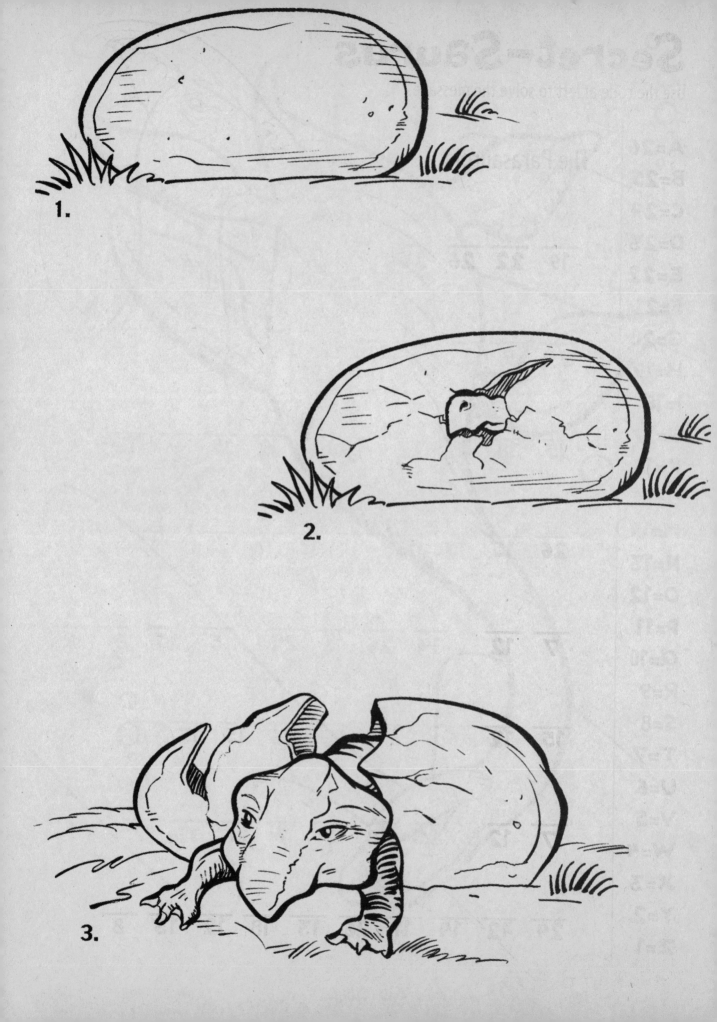

1.

2.

3.

Secret-Saurus

Use the code at left to solve the message.

A=26
B=25
C=24
D=23
E=22
F=21
G=20
H=19
I=18
J=17
K=16
L=15
M=14
N=13
O=12
P=11
Q=10
R=9
S=8
T=7
U=6
V=5
W=4
X=3
Y=2
Z=1

The Parasaurolophus uses its

$\overline{19}$ $\overline{22}$ $\overline{26}$ $\overline{23}$
(HEAD)

$\overline{24}$ $\overline{9}$ $\overline{22}$ $\overline{8}$ $\overline{7}$
(CREST)

$\overline{15}$ $\overline{18}$ $\overline{16}$ $\overline{22}$ $\overline{26}$ $\overline{19}$ $\overline{12}$ $\overline{9}$ $\overline{13}$
(LIKE A HORN)

$\overline{26}$ $\overline{15}$ $\overline{15}$ $\overline{12}$ $\overline{4}$ $\overline{18}$ $\overline{13}$ $\overline{20}$ $\overline{18}$ $\overline{7}$
(ALLOWING IT)

$\overline{7}$ $\overline{12}$ $\overline{14}$ $\overline{26}$ $\overline{16}$ $\overline{22}$ $\overline{5}$ $\overline{22}$ $\overline{9}$ $\overline{2}$
(TO MAKE VERY)

$\overline{15}$ $\overline{12}$ $\overline{6}$ $\overline{23}$ $\overline{24}$ $\overline{26}$ $\overline{15}$ $\overline{15}$ $\overline{8}$
(LOUD CALLS)

$\overline{7}$ $\overline{12}$ $\overline{23}$ $\overline{18}$ $\overline{8}$ $\overline{7}$ $\overline{26}$ $\overline{13}$ $\overline{7}$
(TO DISTANT)

$\overline{24}$ $\overline{12}$ $\overline{14}$ $\overline{11}$ $\overline{26}$ $\overline{13}$ $\overline{18}$ $\overline{12}$ $\overline{13}$ $\overline{8}$
(COMPANIONS)

Which-Saurus

Which picture shows a Plesiosaur? Cross out the items on the list and circle the remaining dinosaur.

Cross Outs:

1. Dinosaurs with long tails
2. Dinosaurs with tiny arms
3. Dinosaurs with bone plates on its back
4. Dinosaurs with wings

Draw-a-Saurus

Use the grid to draw the dinosaur.

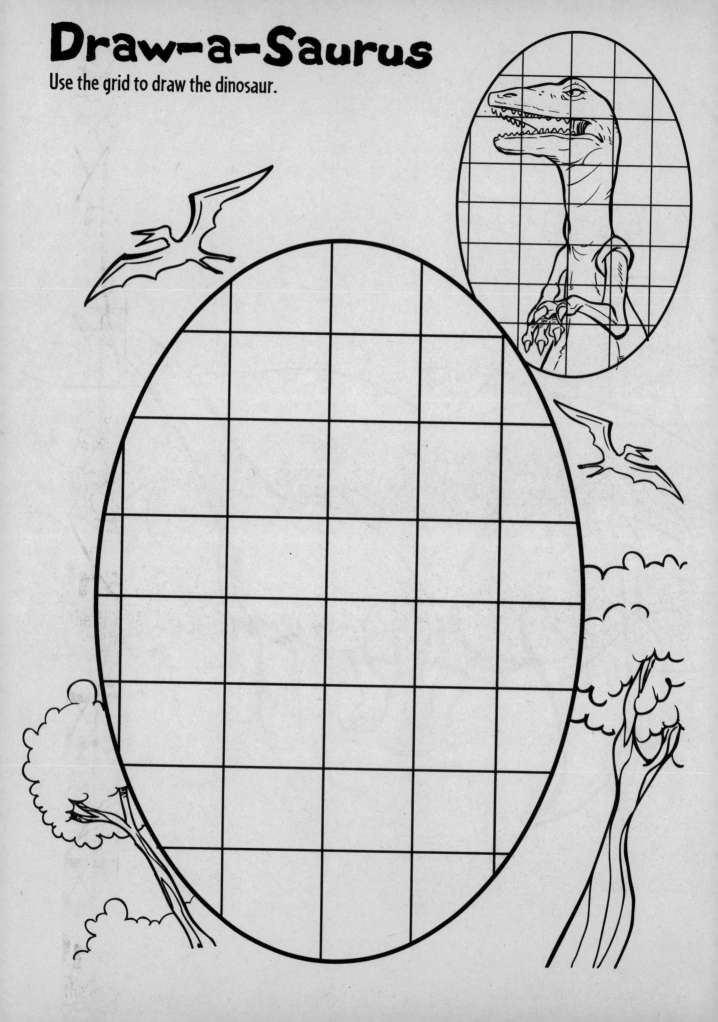

Hidden-Saurus

How many times can you find the word DINOSAUR? Look forwards, backwards, up, down, and diagonally.

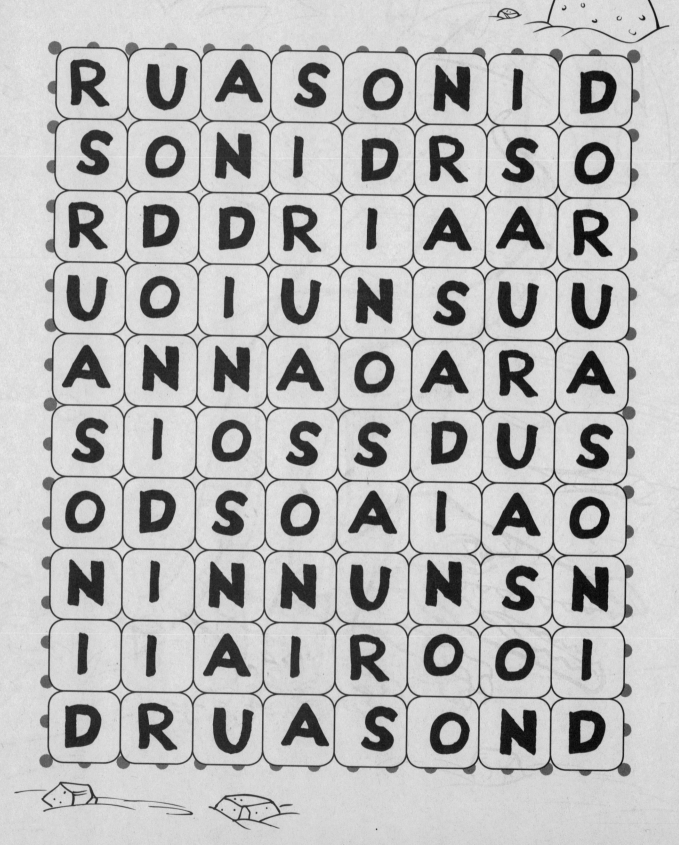

R	U	A	S	O	N	I	D	I	D
S	O	N	I	D	R	S	R	S	O
R	D	D	R	I	A	A	U	O	R
U	O	I	U	N	S	U	U	R	U
A	N	N	A	O	A	R	A	A	S
S	I	O	S	S	D	U	S	A	S
O	D	S	O	A	I	A	O	N	N
N	I	N	N	U	N	S	N	I	A
I	I	A	I	R	O	O	I	D	R
D	R	U	A	S	O	N	D	N	D

Mirror-Saurus

Hold this page up to a mirror to read the secret message.

The wings on a
Pterodactyl could be up
to 40 feet long.

Puzzle-Saurus

Which piece is the missing piece of the puzzle?

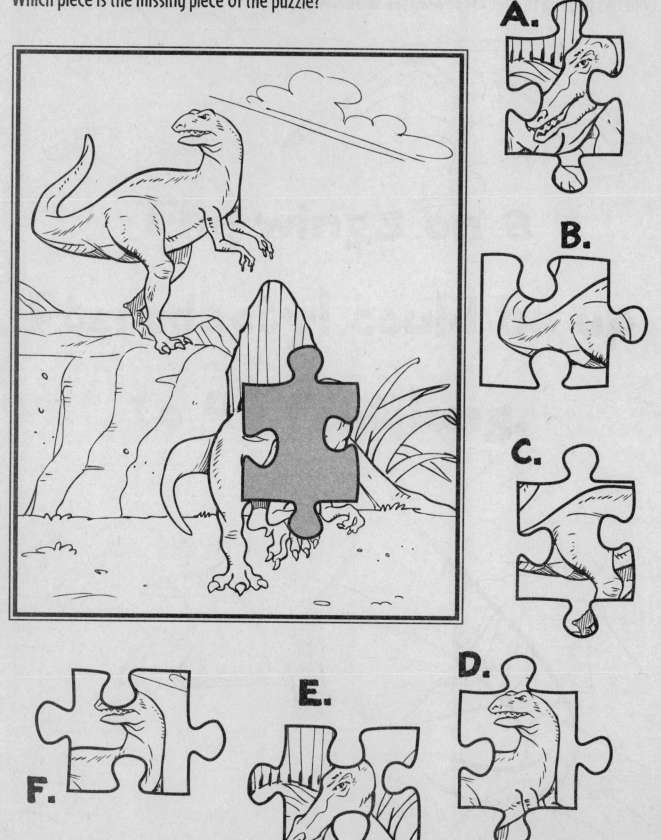

Differ-A-Saurus

One of these dinosaurs is not like the others. Can you figure
out which one doesn't belong?

Path-Odon

Follow the lines and write the letters in the boxes to discover what bird was the size of the smallest dinosaur.

Dot-to-Dot-ylus

Connect the dots to discover a ferocious dinosaur!

Tic-Tac-Saurus

Play this game with one of your friends.

Shadow-saurus

Match the dinosaur to his shadow.

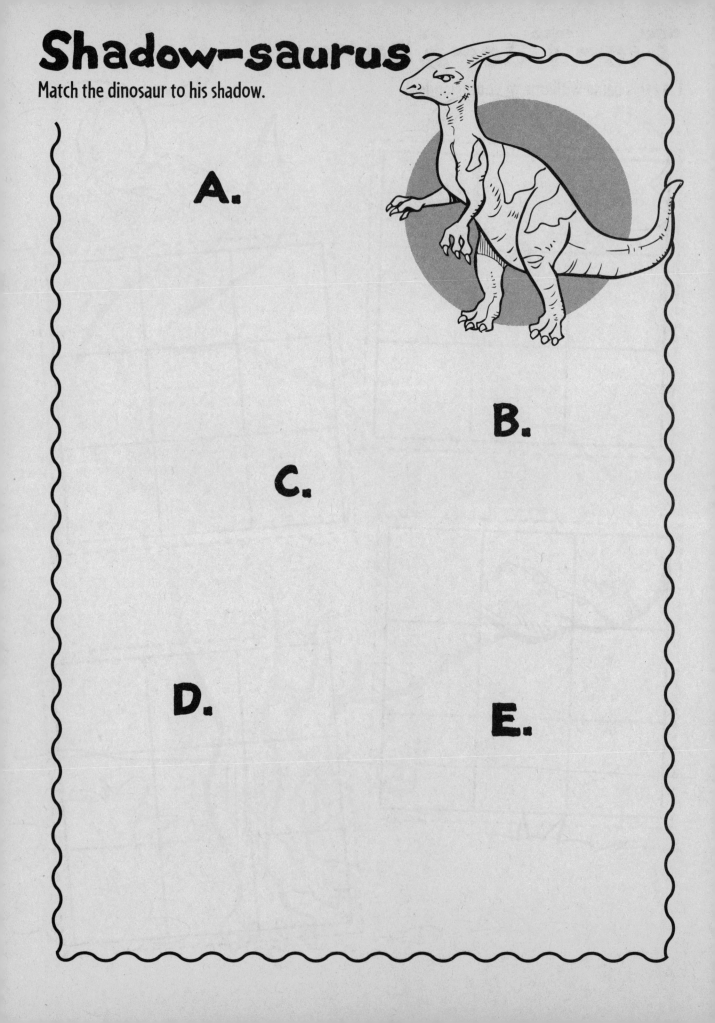

A.

B.

C.

D.

E.

Spot-A-Saurus

Can you spot the 6 differences between this picture and the one on the following page?

Follow-A-Saurus

Follow the dinosaur in the direction it's facing until you reach the finish.

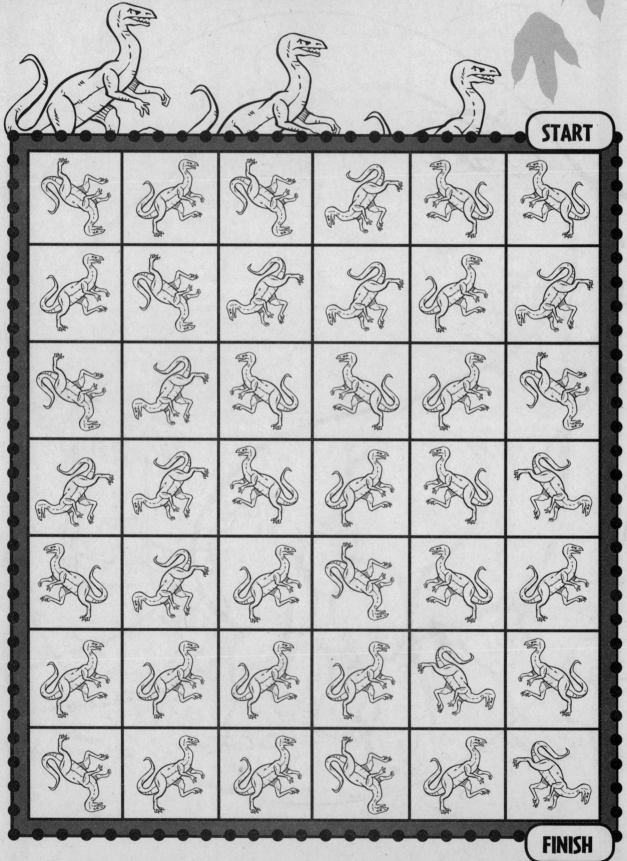

START

FINISH

Decorate-a-Saurus

Decorate the dinosaur and color it in!

Maze-A-Saurus

Help the dinosaur get through the maze to find her baby.

How many words can you make out of the letters in

Triceratops?

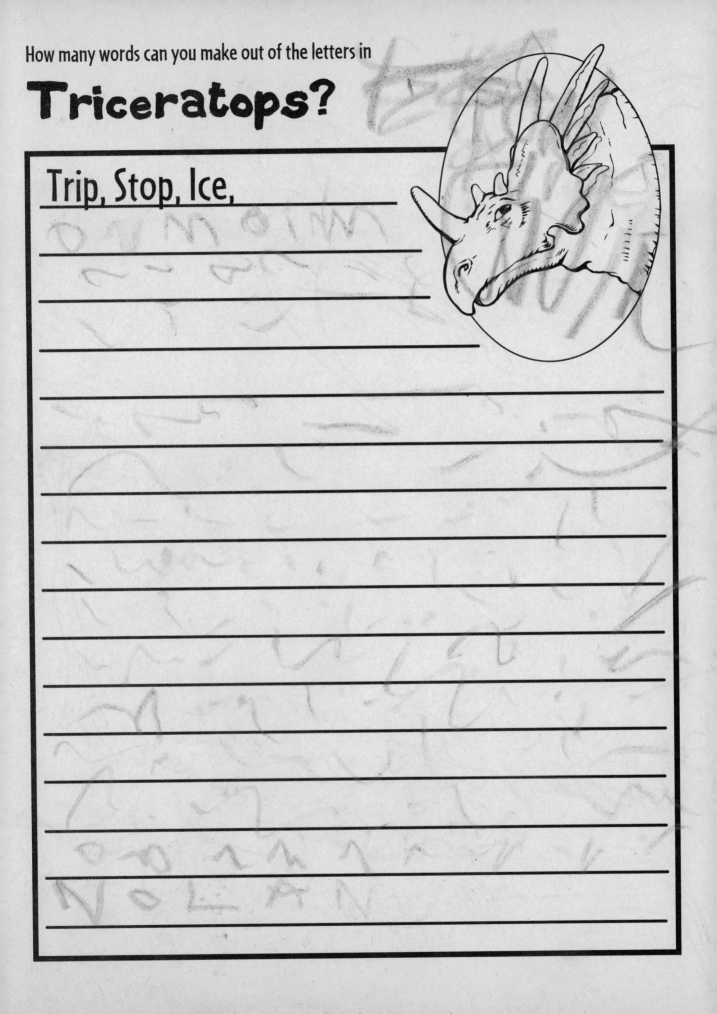

Trip, Stop, Ice,

Tell-a-Saurus

Write a story of what you would do if you met a dinosaur!

_____

_____

_____

_____

_____

_____

_____

_____

_____

_____

_____

_____

Draw-a-Saurus

Use the space to draw and color your favorite dinosaur!

My favorite dinosaur!

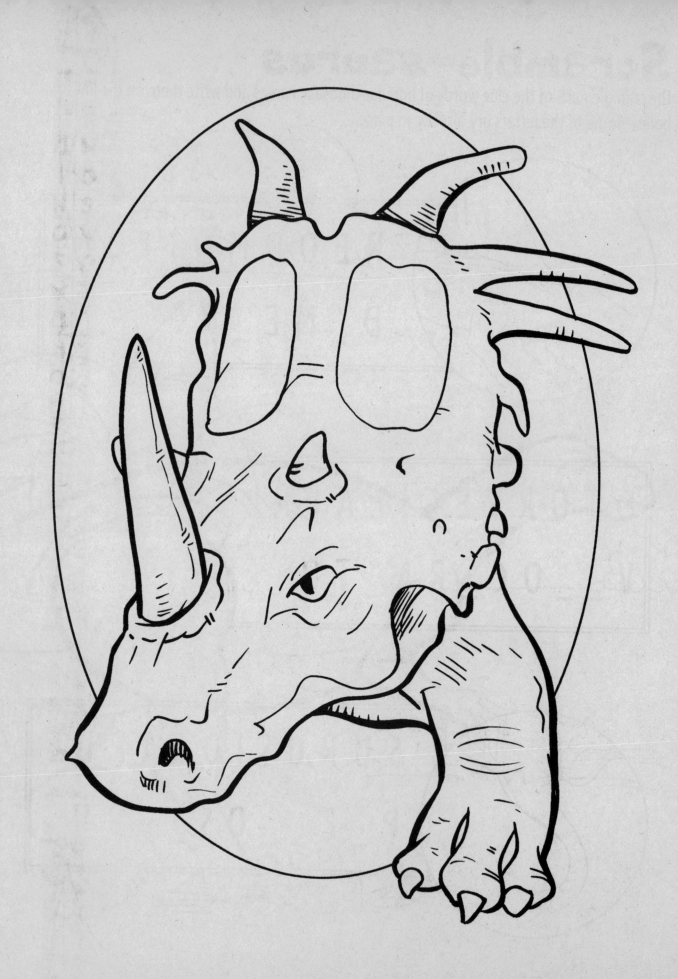

Scramble-saurus

Unscramble each of the clue words of popular dinosaur names and write them on the lines below. Some of the letters are already in place.

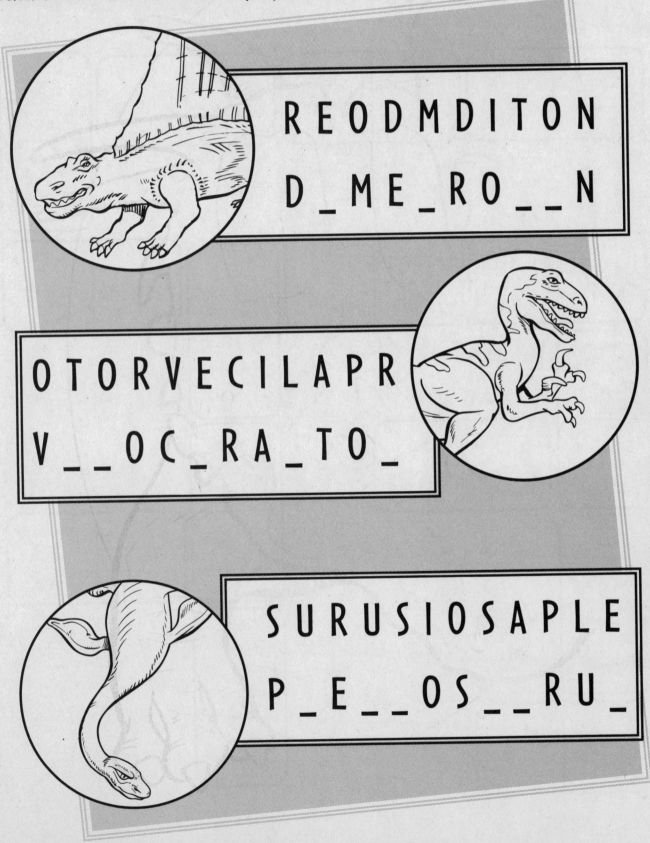

REODMDITON

D _ M E _ R O _ _ N

OTORVECILAPR

V _ _ O C _ R A _ T O _

SURUSIOSAPLE

P _ E _ _ O S _ _ R U _

Domino-Saurus

The symbol on each domino matches the domino next to it except for one.
Circle the piece that doesn't match on either side.

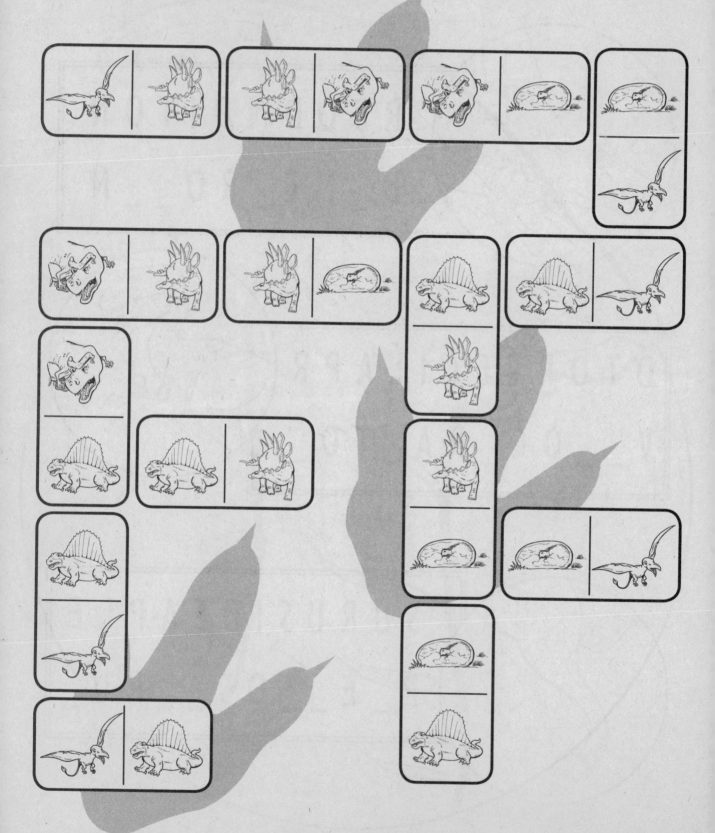

Search-A-Saurus

Find the words in the grid below. Search up, down, left, right, backwards and diagonally.

ALLOSAURUS	DIMORPHODON	STEGOSAURUS
BRACHIOSAURUS	PLESIOSAURUS	TRICERATOPS
CEARADACTYLUS	PTERODACTYLS	VELOCIRAPTOR

```
L S T E G O S A U R U S S S H
N O D O H P R O M I D K U U F
S A C U L B H I P E A Z R R O
W G X E K R V D T W T U U U G
X W M J A F J Y E N R K A A U
W J K R T R G L R P I B S S N
D D X T M M A V O A C M O O A
X B U C B Z Q D D H E N I L N
B R A C H I O S A U R U S L B
U Y W K Y G C X C C A G E A Y
H U N V W I C U T D T K L R V
V D D K J Z R B Y Z O Y P R D
E H Y U C C B D L L P I L V Y
T G V Y E D U C S R S A K U U
R O T P A R I C O L E V G N S
```

Count-A-Saurus

Count how many dinosaurs there are. Write the number in the box below.

Order-Saurus

Put the boxes to the right in order by placing the correct letters in the boxes to the left.

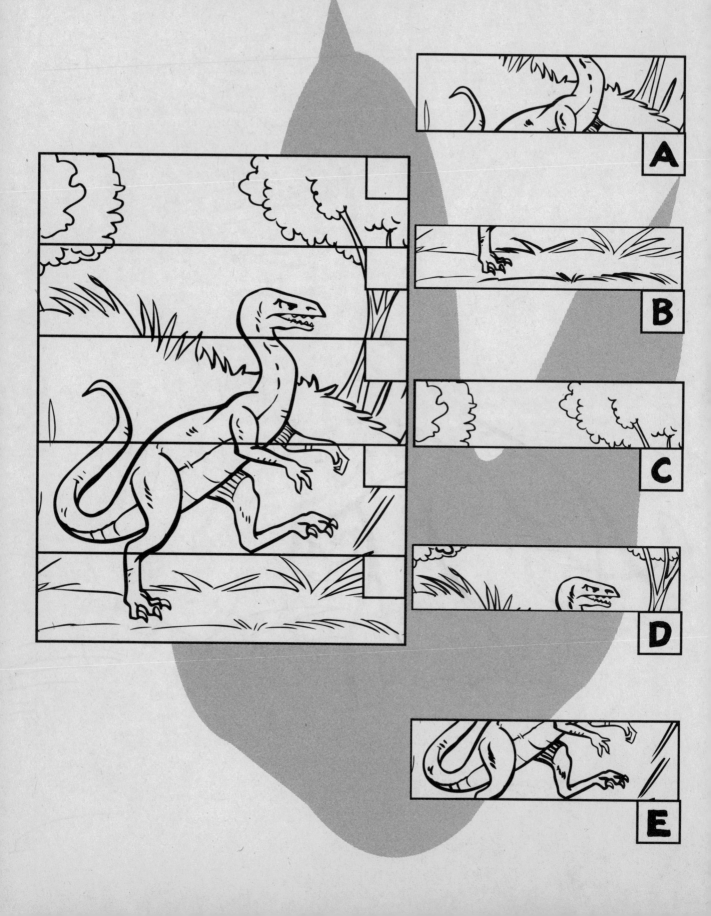

Match-A-Saurus

Find the two matching dinosaurs.

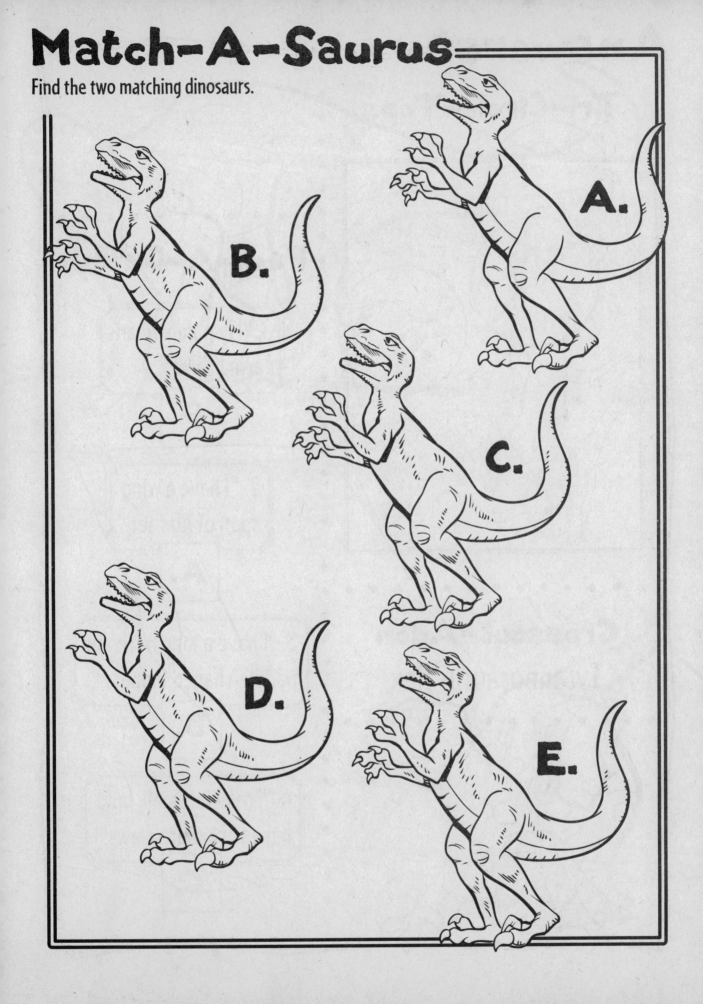

Answers:

Tri-Circle-Tops

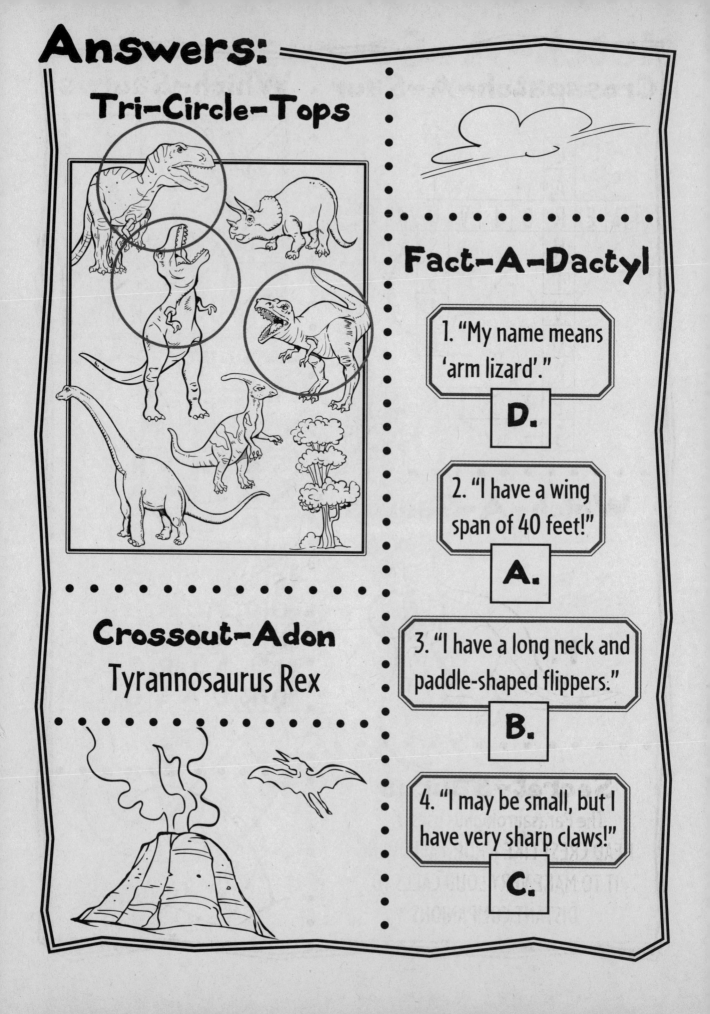

Crossout-Adon

Tyrannosaurus Rex

Fact-A-Dactyl

1. "My name means 'arm lizard'."

D.

2. "I have a wing span of 40 feet!"

A.

3. "I have a long neck and paddle-shaped flippers."

B.

4. "I may be small, but I have very sharp claws!"

C.

Crosspatch-A-Saur

```
    C
    A   F
H E R B I V O R E S
    N   O
    I   S
    V   S
    O   I
    R   L
    E
    S X T I N C T
    S
```

Which-Saurus

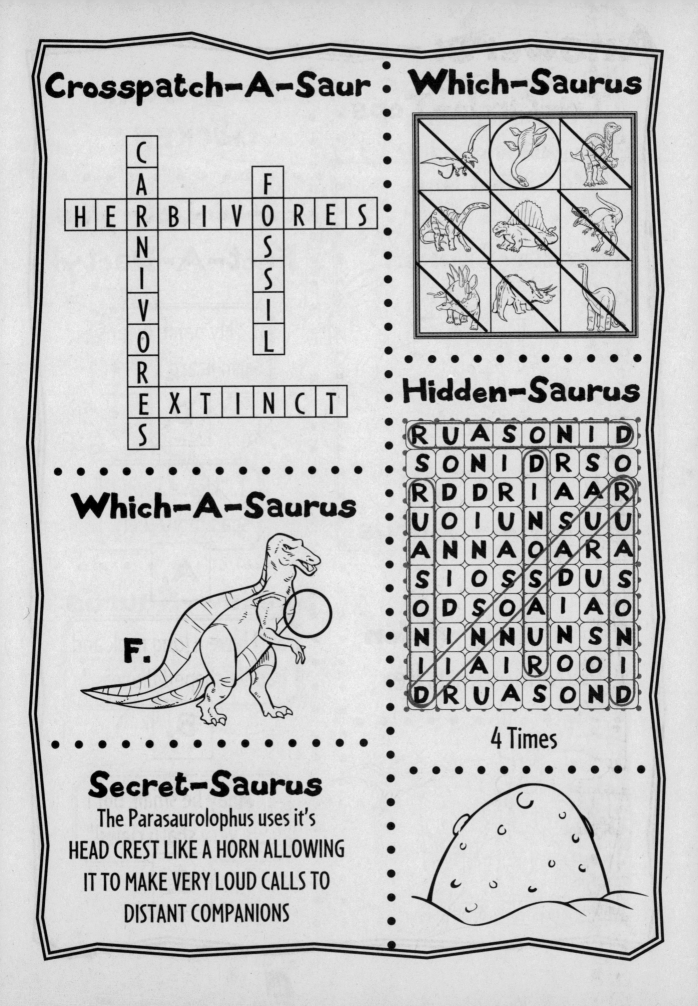

Which-A-Saurus

F.

Secret-Saurus

The Parasaurolophus uses it's
HEAD CREST LIKE A HORN ALLOWING
IT TO MAKE VERY LOUD CALLS TO
DISTANT COMPANIONS

Hidden-Saurus

```
R U A S O N I D
S O N I D R S O
R D D R I A A R
U O I U N S U U
A N N A O A R A
A S I O S S D U S
O D S O A I A O
N I N N U N S N
I I A I R O O I
D R U A S O N D
```

4 Times

Mirror-Saurus
The wings on a Pterodactyl could be up to 40 feet long.

Puzzle-Saurus

A.

Differ-A-Saurus

Walks on two feet instead of four.

Path-Odon
CHICKEN

Dot-to-Dot-ylus

Shadow-Saurus

A.

Spot-A-Saurus

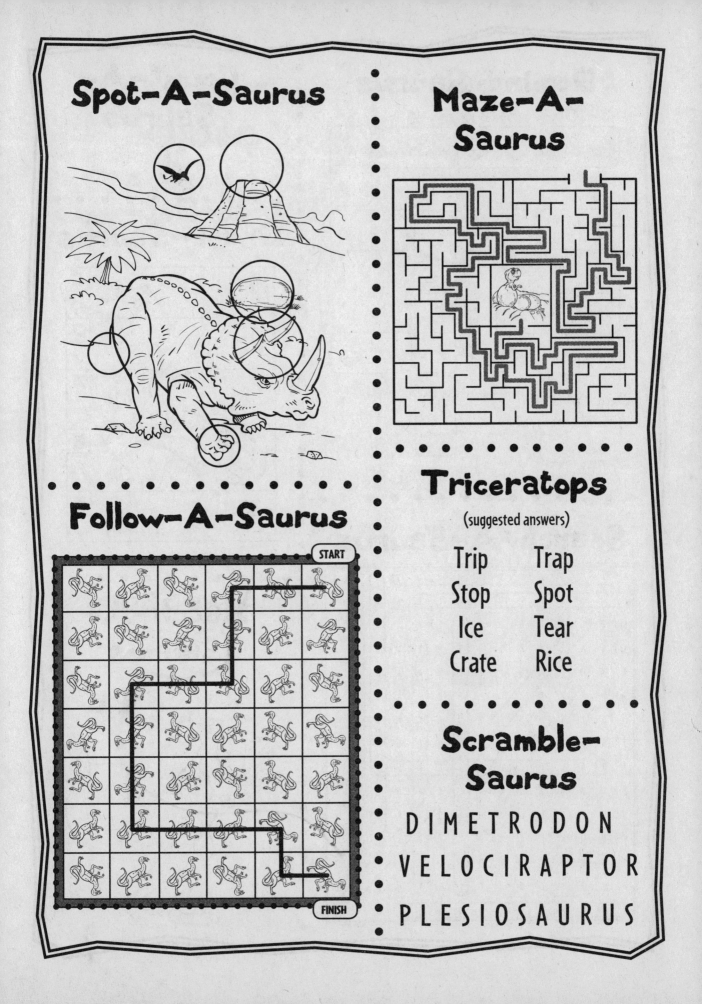

Maze-A-Saurus

Follow-A-Saurus

START

FINISH

Triceratops

(suggested answers)

Trip   Trap
Stop   Spot
Ice   Tear
Crate   Rice

Scramble-Saurus

DIMETRODON

VELOCIRAPTOR

PLESIOSAURUS

Domino-Saurus

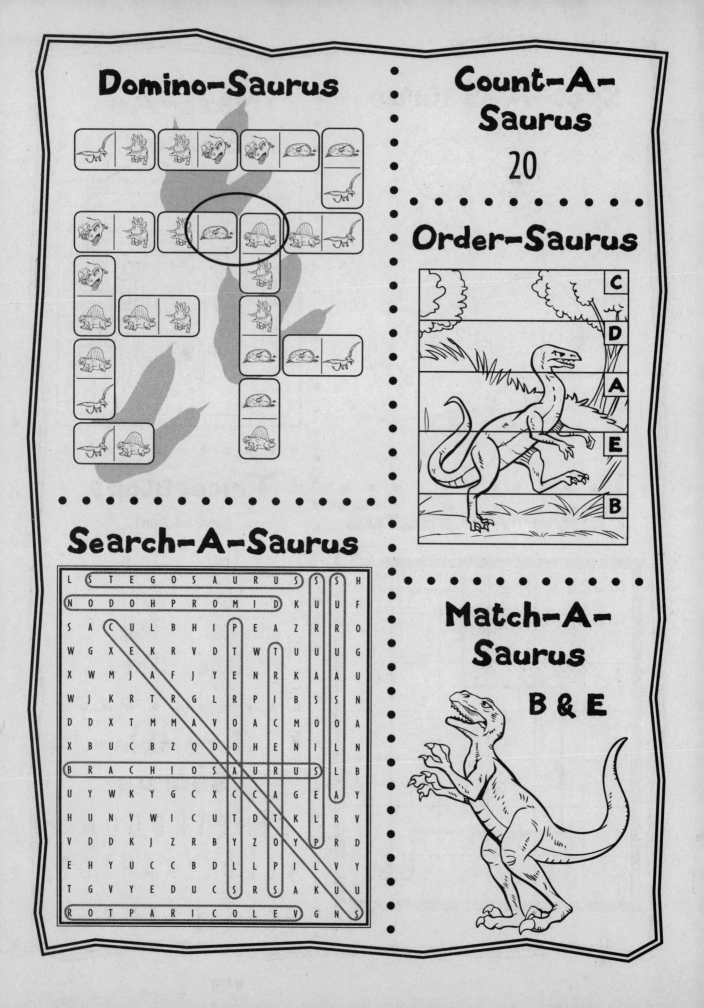

Count-A-Saurus
20

Order-Saurus

C
D
A
E
B

Search-A-Saurus

```
L S T E G O S A U R U S S S H
N O D O H P R O M I D K U F
S A C U L B H I P E A Z R R O
W G X E K R V D T W T U U G
X W M J A F J Y E N R K U N
W J K R T R G L R P I B S U N
D D X T M M A V O A C M O A
X B U C B Z Q D H E N I N L
B R A C H I O S A U R U S L B
U Y W K Y G C X C A G E A Y
H U N V W I C U T D T K L R V
V D D K J Z R B Y Z O Y P R D
E H Y U C C B D L L P I L V Y
T G V V Y E D U C S R S A K U U
R O T P A R I C O L E V G N S
```

Match-A-Saurus
B & E